NURTURING YOUR FIRST PET

A comprehensive guide for new pet parents, covering everything from preparation to lifelong care to ensure a happy and healthy life for their furry friends.

Marcy Brown

Table of contents

Introduction

Getting a pet is like getting a new family member. Although they provide happiness, company, and unconditional affection, pets also come with a number of duties. Taking care of a pet involves time, effort, and concern for their wellbeing, just like parenting a kid.

In order to guarantee a happy and healthy life for their animal companions even before taking on the responsibility, every pet owner should accept the fundamental principles covered in this book as we dive into the realm of responsible pet care.

Selecting the Ideal Pet
Spend some time learning about the specific requirements,

attributes, temperament, and qualities of the pet you are thinking about before making such a significant choice as selecting a pet. A dog might be the ideal friend if you lead an active lifestyle and take pleasure in outdoor pursuits. However, a cat could be a better choice if you'd rather have a low-maintenance, independent pet.

While cats and dogs are cherished companions, discovering the world of alternative pets may result in profound and rewarding bonds with creatures of all sizes and forms. Every pet adds a certain charm and happiness to your life, whether it's by cuddling with a soft bunny, listening to a birdchirp, or taking in the breathtaking beauty of an aquarium.

Every breed or species has unique needs when it comes to training, grooming, and exercise. Having a clear understanding of these aspects will enable you to choose a pet that fits your needs and lifestyle.

Providing a healthy diet

You may be surprised to learn how much more crucial a proper diet is. Although it would be tempting to offer your dog leftovers from the dinner table, doing so might potentially cause health problems for them. Every pet has different nutritional needs, so it's best to speak with a veterinarian to figure out the best kind of food and serving amount for your pet depending on breed, age, and activity level.

They will remain in shape, maintain a healthy weight, and be less vulnerable to health issues if they eat a balanced diet. Keep a close eye on their weight and modify their diet as necessary. Make sure there is always access to fresh, clean water.

Frequent veterinary care

Although it may seem like your pet is unbeatable, they are not. Whenever they cough or display other minor symptoms, it's crucial to monitor them closely and promptly take them to the veterinarian. Don't put off a visit. A cough may indicate a respiratory ailment that poses a serious risk to your pet.

Pets need regular medical checkups to be healthy, just as people do. Frequent veterinary checkups aid in the early detection of any health concerns, preventing them from developing into more serious ones. Maintaining the healthiest possible condition for your pet also requires regular dental care, flea and tick preventative treatments, and vaccinations.

Appropriate instruction and socialization

Socialization and training are two other areas that are often disregarded. It's a frequent misunderstanding to assume that your pet will automatically adjust to your lifestyle. The secret to maintaining a happy connection with your pet is proper socialization and training. A happy and well-behaved pet is the result of spending time teaching them enjoyable skills, housebreaking, and basic obedience training.

Your pet will gain confidence, have less fear, and have fewer possible behavioral problems as a result of being socialized with humans and other animals. Additionally, it could be a win-win situation where you connect with other animal enthusiasts, learn more about them via PhoneHistory, and form friendships with like-minded locals.

Establishing a secure environment

Thousands of pets unintentionally swallow tiny, inedible items that are put within reach each year. The number of emergency visits to the veterinarian to address such incidents would significantly decrease if more houses containing these animals were pet-proofed.

Proofing your home is one of the most important aspects of safe pet care. Take out anything dangerous that your pet may swallow or tangle with. Give your pet a special place to play, relax, and relieve themselves. Put up gates to keep people from escaping, and don't leave them alone in potentially hazardous circumstances.

Frequent physical activity and mental challenges

When busy pet owners of energetic dogs get home from work, they sometimes discover that their dog's enthusiasm has taken the form of undesired habits like excessive barking and furniture chewing. But the animal isn't at fault.

For your pet to stay healthy, daily exercise and mental stimulation are essential. Dogs need entertainment, engaging activities, and frequent walks to maintain their physical condition and burn off energy. Cats also enjoy playing with toys that appeal to their instincts. Getting your pet involved in different activities helps them stay mentally and physically healthy, as well as lessen stress.

Tidying up and being sanitary

Maintaining your pet's health and comfort requires regular grooming. The demands for grooming an animal differ depending on its species. For example, dogs may need frequent washing, nail cutting, and combing. While they can groom themselves rather well, cats sometimes may need help. In addition to keeping your pet looking their best, proper grooming helps shield them against infections and skin problems.

Recognition and microchipping

Having your pet properly identified may significantly improve the likelihood of a joyful reunion in the event that they go missing. Make sure your pet wears a collar with a visible identification tag displaying your contact information. You should also think about microchipping your pet, which involves implanting a tiny, permanent identifying chip under their skin. If your pet is lost without a collar or tag, microchips significantly increase the chances of their identification.

Impact on the Environment

Having a responsible pet involves more than just your house. Examine the effects that your pet's care has on the environment. When feasible, use biodegradable trash bags, environmentally friendly pet supplies, and pet food that is obtained responsibly. To keep your neighborhood safe and tidy, always pick up after your pet while out on walks and dispose of trash appropriately.

Being Ready for Emergencies

To protect your pet and keep them safe, be ready for anything. Assemble an emergency supply kit with necessities such as water, food, medicine, and medical documents. Prepare a strategy for taking your pet with you if there are any crises or natural catastrophes. Furthermore, choose a dependable friend or relative who will take care of your pet in the event that you are momentarily unable to.

Dedication and forbearance

Oliver, a timid and scared rescue cat, is one of the most endearing instances of devotion and endurance. He hid for days after moving into his new house and refused to talk to his new family. But with persistent love and gentle tolerance, he came out of his shell and became a cherished and loving part of the family.

The two main components of proper pet ownership are **dedication** and **perseverance**. Certain pets could need some time to become used to their new environment, particularly if they have had difficult experiences in the past. They will develop deep trust and affection for your commitment to their well-being, as well as your understanding and kind guidance, which will make them feel safe and loved.

The advantages of owning a pet

Numerous studies have been conducted on the relationship between dogs and human health for at least 40 years, and they have identified a number of unexpected advantages.

Numerous approaches exist for pets to enhance their wellbeing. Pet ownership provides many advantages that may improve your life in many ways, but it also entails substantial obligations.

Emotional support and companionship

Pet ownership's companionship and emotional support are

among the most significant advantages. They may lessen feelings of despair and loneliness and provide unconditional affection.

Emotional relationship: An owner and pet may have an extraordinarily close relationship. Pets often pick up on their owners' feelings and provide consolation when they're stressed or depressed.

Reduced stress: Research has shown that spending time with dogs may lower stress levels. A relaxing effect may be achieved by petting a dog or cat, since it releases endorphins and lowers cortisol levels.

Enhanced Happiness: Having a pet may greatly improve your general happiness and well-being, since they offer pleasure and laughter.

Advantages for Physical Health

Improving one's physical health is another benefit of pet ownership. Frequent pet engagement promotes physical activity and has been associated with a number of health advantages.

Greater exercise: Because dogs, in particular, need to play and go for regular walks, their owners often engage in greater physical activity as well. This may help with weight management and cardiovascular health.

Reduced Blood Pressure: According to research, pet owners often have lower blood pressure compared to those without pets. The routine of taking care of a pet, as well as its soothing presence, contribute to this impact.

Enhanced Immune System: According to some studies,

early-life pet exposure may help boost immunity and lower the incidence of allergies and asthma.

Social Communication

Additionally, pets may act as social catalysts, promoting a sense of community and assisting with interpersonal connections.

Meeting New People: Taking a dog on a walk or going to a dog park may introduce you to other pet owners, which can lead to friendship and socializing possibilities.

Strengthening Relationships: Because pet owners share the duties and rewards of pet keeping, pets may strengthen family bonds. Fostering a pet together may make family ties stronger.

Community Involvement: You may get more involved in the community by taking part in pet-related events, such as training sessions, pet exhibitions, or volunteer work at animal shelters.

Advantages for the Mind and Cognition

Engaging with pets may also improve mental and cognitive well-being, especially for young people and the elderly.

Cognitive Stimulation: Playing and training dogs requires you to think critically and solve problems, which might help to keep your mind sharp.

Benefits of Pet Therapy: People with dementia, autism, and mental health disorders often get pet therapy. An animal's presence may be soothing and beneficial for enhancing cognitive performance.

Possibilities for Education: Taking care of a pet instills in kids values of responsibility, empathy, and nurturing. Additionally, it offers possibilities for learning about the biology and behavior of animals.

Pets may enhance your physical health in three ways.
Pets are more than just devoted friends. The health of the heart and brain may also be preserved by them.

safeguarding cardiovascular health
High levels of inflammation may be caused by ongoing stress, which can harm blood vessels. Stress also causes the body to overproduce cortisol and adrenaline, which raise blood pressure and heart rate.

Pets, however, may lessen stress
When you touch or stroke an animal, your brain produces oxytocin. This hormone reduces stress and makes you want to spend more time with your loved ones. Additionally, pets might encourage you to engage in other heart-healthy activities, such as getting adequate exercise.

Cognitive decline is slowing down
The evidence on the benefits of pet ownership for cognitive health is mixed. According to 2023 research, older individuals with pets for more than five years outperformed older persons without dogs on routine cognitive tests. The study was unable to determine if or why having a pet may have improved test performance. However, as some probable contributing causes, the research authors noted potential pet impacts such as higher oxytocin, improved physical activity, a reduced incidence of high blood pressure, and lower stress.

Our pets depend on us, and it's nice to be needed.
Maintaining routines can help you feel more in control of your

life and find your center, especially during stressful and anxious periods.

Enhanced ability to tolerate stress
As was previously said, oxytocin is released when you cuddle with a pet, which helps lower stress. In one study, college students reported feeling less worried before final examinations after spending ten minutes engaging with a dog.

Decreased isolation
Stressors like loneliness and social isolation raise the risk of dementia, heart disease, and stroke, among other illnesses.
But having a pet might make us feel less alone.

Participants in a study of 448 individuals conducted during the COVID-19 pandemic lockdowns answered online questionnaires that assessed their mental health. The results showed that pet owners fared better during lockdowns than non-proprietors did in terms of adjusting to isolation. Additionally, those who had dogs performed better on tests of happiness and wellbeing.

It's interesting to note that having a pet doesn't always mean that someone will feel less alone. Alternatives, such as pet robots, which are suitable for those unable to care for a live animal, may also help safeguard mental health. In one tiny study, robotic dogs or cats were offered as companions to elderly residents with dementia who were at a residential care facility. Like stuffed animals, the animal robots were made of artificial fur and could respond to touch and sound by meowing, barking, and wagging their tails. The research participants' scores on sadness and loneliness assessments decreased after a six-week period of cohabitation with these dogs.

Benefits of pet ownership for social health
Consider what occurs when you take a dog for a walk or post a picture of your cat on social media.
Your pet makes others feel quite comfortable approaching you, which may improve your relationships with other local residents.

Better physical and mental health may be a result of this increase in social health. Heart disease, dementia, and depression are more common in those who are lonely or socially isolated. Conversely, those who experience more social connectedness often have longer, healthier lives.

Pets are not a cure-all.
Pets provide several health advantages, much like pharmaceutical drugs, but they may also have unfavorable side effects.
You may feel more at ease when your dogs sleep on your bed. However, dogs may also scurry around throughout the night and keep you awake. Pets age as much as people do, which may result in costly veterinary care and ultimately bereavement. It might be challenging to take care of a pet if you're less mobile; food and litter bags can be heavy to handle, and dogs need to go outside to relieve themselves.

So, before introducing a new pet into your home, it is important to understand the obligations and benefits of pet ownership. Understanding the many physical, psychological, and social advantages of owning a pet, along with the daily maintenance and long-term commitment needed, will help you make an educated choice that will result in a happy and satisfying relationship with your companion. In addition to bringing us happiness, affection, and company, pets also help us learn important life skills like empathy and responsibility.

Chapter one: How to Pick a Pet That Fits Your Lifestyle

Choosing to adopt a pet is a thrilling and fulfilling choice. However, in order to guarantee a happy and satisfying connection, selecting the ideal pet for your lifestyle is essential. We will discuss the things to think about while choosing a pet in this chapter, such as your living circumstances, degree of activity, availability of time, and personal preferences. You may make an educated choice and choose the ideal pet partner that enriches your life with happiness and company by according to these tips.

Evaluate your current living situation:

Take into account your home's layout and available area in addition to its size. If your apartment is smaller, think about whether your pet can exercise and explore the parks or green areas nearby. Additionally, consider if your living arrangement permits particular pets, such those that need specialized habitat settings or outside cages.

Assess Your Degree of Activity:

Consider your favorite leisure activities in addition to your regular routine. You could be more inclined to a more active and adventurous pet, such as a dog, if you like hiking, camping, or other outdoor activities. However, a low-energy creature like a cat or a tiny pet that can be kept in an enclosure can be a better fit if you prefer peaceful indoor pursuits.

Think About Your Time Commitment:

Think about the long-term commitment necessary as well as the amount of time needed for daily care. Certain pets—like dogs, for example—benefit greatly from human companionship and may get anxious when left alone for long stretches of time. Think about whether you can give your pet the time and care they need if you have a hectic schedule or travel regularly. On the other hand, other pets—like specific fish or reptiles—need less attention and are more appropriate for those with busy schedules.

Investigate Species and Breeds:

Examine the unique temperaments, activity demands, and grooming requirements of various breeds and species while doing your study. Think about whether you would rather have a more autonomous pet or one that is more social and trainable. Certain breeds could be more suited for single people or couples, while others might be ideal for families with young children. Making an educated choice will be made easier if you are aware of the distinctive characteristics of various breeds and kinds.

Sensitivities and Allergies:

It's important to pick a pet that is hypoallergenic, or less likely to provoke allergies, if you or anybody else in your home has allergies or sensitivities. Although no pet is totally hypoallergenic, certain breeds have hair instead of fur or create less allergens than others, which lowers the likelihood of allergic responses. To determine whether you will have any adverse responses in advance, think about going to see friends or relatives who own the kind of pet you are interested in.

Aspects of Finance:

Consider the monetary obligations associated with pet ownership. Think about recurring costs like food, tidiness, vet care, shots, and pet insurance in addition to the adoption or purchase price. Your budget may be impacted by the special food requirements or ongoing grooming demands of some dogs. It's crucial to make sure you have enough money to meet your pet's demands.

Long-Term Commitment:

Consider your long-term goals and how your pet will fit into them. Think about significant life events like changing careers, relocating, or beginning a family. In the long term, owning a pet comes with responsibilities, so be sure you're ready for the stability and security that pets demand in your household.

Adoption:

Think about obtaining a pet via adoption from a shelter or rescue group. You provide an animal in need a loving home by doing this. Furthermore, shelters often have a large variety of mixed-breed and purebred dogs available, providing you with plenty of options. The cost of adopting a pet is usually less than that of purchasing one from a breeder, and many shelters provide free initial vaccines as well as spaying and neutering services.

Chapter Two: Pet Types

Selecting the ideal pet is a big choice that has to be well thought out, taking into account a number of variables such as your living situation, lifestyle, and personal preferences. Every type of pet has unique requirements and traits. This is a comprehensive look at the many kinds of pets you can think about, including common breeds, maintenance needs, and other relevant information.

Canines:

Because of their adaptability, loyalty, and companionship, dogs are among the most popular pet animals. But because every breed is unique in terms of temperament and maintenance needs, some types are better suited for first-time pet owners than others.

Well-liked Breeds for Beginners

1. Labrador Retriever: Labradors are excellent with families and kids because of their gregarious and extroverted personalities. They are both easy to teach and clever.

2. Golden Retriever: Labradors and Golden Retrievers share the trait of being kind, amiable, and very trainable. They require frequent grooming and exercise.

3. Beagle: Beagles are small to medium-sized dogs with an inquisitive and amiable disposition. While they are fantastic with children, they might be a little obstinate during training.

4. Poodle (Miniature and Standard): Poodles are hypoallergenic and very clever, which makes them a good choice for those with allergies. They must be groomed on a regular basis.

5. Shih Tzu: These little dogs are affectionate and make wonderful apartment pets. Although they are usually low-maintenance, they do need to be groomed on a regular basis.

Details and maintenance are required.

Tiny Dogs: They are suitable for homes with smaller living areas, such as flats. Although they often need less exercise, they may be more vulnerable to some health problems.

Medium Dogs: Because of their adaptability, these dogs can live in both apartments and homes with yards. They need mental stimulation and frequent exercise.

Big Dogs: are ideal for houses with backyards. They need a lot of exercise and room to roam around. In addition to having shorter lifespans, large dogs may also be more susceptible to certain health problems.

Felines :

Cats are an excellent choice for those who lead busy lives or live in smaller places since they are autonomous and often need less upkeep than dogs.

Well-liked Breeds for Beginners

1. British Shorthair: Because of their minimal maintenance requirements and laid-back disposition.

2. Siamese: Siamese cats are talkative, gregarious, and loving. They may establish close relationships with their owners and enjoy socializing.

3. Ragdoll: Due to their soft nature and tolerance, ragdolls are wonderful companions for households with young children. They are renowned for having silky fur and stunning blue eyes.

4. Maine Coon: One of the biggest breeds of domestic cats, Maine Coons get along well with kids and other animals and are lively and amiable.

5. Persian: The Persian breed of cats is peaceful and kind. Their lengthy hair means that they need to be groomed often.

Outdoor vs. Indoor Felines

Indoor cats are less likely to become sick or injured, generally speaking. More playtime and excitement are necessary for indoor cats to avoid boredom and obesity.

Outdoor Cats: They may roam around and exercise in their natural habitat, but they run the risk of becoming sick from infections, traffic, and predators. A catio or safe outdoor area might provide a middle ground.

Small Mammals

Small mammals may make excellent pets for people who prefer creatures that don't require as much meticulous care or have limited space such as; *Rabbits, Hamsters, and Guinea Pigs*

I. Hamsters: Ideal for children and small areas, hamsters are tiny and require little care. They need a lot of bedding in their cage, a wheel for exercise, and frequent cleaning.

II. Guinea Pigs: gregarious and sociable, guinea pigs love company, whether it comes from other guinea pigs or their owners. They need a large cage with plenty of hay and fresh vegetables.

III. Rabbits: Clever and gregarious, they can be housebroken and allowed unrestricted access to the house as long as they are supervised. For good digestion and dental health, they need plenty of hay, fresh veggies, and a spacious enclosure.

Aegean

Birds may be quite fulfilling as pets because they provide company and, in some situations, can imitate human speech like *Canaries, Cockatiels, and Parakeets.*

I. Parakeets (Budgies) are a great choice for first-time bird owners because they are small, colorful, and generally require little maintenance. They need socialization, well-balanced food, and a large cage.

II. Canaries: Unlike other birds, canaries are more aloof while being recognized for their lovely songs. They need water, new food, and a clean cage.

III. Cockatiels: These amicable, medium-sized birds may be taught to imitate noises. They need frequent contact, a roomy cage, and toys to keep their minds active.

Fish

 A fish could be a peaceful and eye-catching addition to your house. They need an aquatic habitat that is kept up to date. There are *Saltwater and Freshwater*

Freshwater fish are more tolerant of novice errors and easier to care for. Tetras, bettas, and goldfish are popular species. For freshwater tanks, water quality monitoring and regular water changes are required.

Saltwater Fish: More difficult since they need certain salinity and water conditions. They have a greater assortment of vibrant species, such as angelfish and clownfish. Seawater tanks need to be carefully maintained and observed.

Reptiles

Although they may make interesting pets, reptiles often need certain environmental conditions to survive such as Lizards, and Turtles etc

Turtles: UVB illumination, basking spaces, and suitable tanks with water purification are necessary for both aquatic and terrestrial turtles. They are a long-term commitment, since they may survive for many decades.

Lizards: Iguanas, geckos, and bearded dragons are all common types of lizards. They need certain nutrition, UVB illumination, humidity, and temperature settings.

Selecting the Ideal Pet

Finding the ideal pet for you means aligning its demands and features with your personality and way of life.

Assigning Pets to Characters, for example:

Active Individuals: Dogs with a lot of energy, such as retrievers or herding types, can be a suitable fit.

Busy Professionals: Fish, cats, or tiny animals that don't need as much care all the time could work.

Families with Children: Ragdolls, Labrador Retrievers, and Golden Retrievers are good breeds to have since they are tolerant and kind.

Allergy Sufferers: Consider hypoallergenic dogs, such as poodles or Siberian cats, as well as other breeds.

Age Factors: Juvenile vs. Adult Pets

 Young Pets: Although they are cute, puppies and kittens need a lot of care and training. They may form close bonds with their owners and be more adaptive.

Older Pets: If you're looking for a more steady companion, older pets may be a suitable fit since they're often already trained and less energetic. Adopting mature dogs may also prevent fatalities.

Medical and Genetic Factors to Consider

Research Breeds: Choose a breed with fewer hereditary disorders by learning about the typical health problems connected to a certain breed.

Adopt from Reputable Sources: Make sure the pet originates from a reliable source that places a high priority on health and appropriate care, whether it be breeders, shelters, or rescues.

Regular Veterinary Care: To keep an eye on and preserve your pet's health, schedule routine vet appointments and budget for any unexpected medical costs.

A careful evaluation of your tastes, lifestyle, and the particular requirements of the pet is necessary when choosing the ideal companion. You may make an educated choice that will result in a fulfilling and peaceful connection with your new companion by being aware of the traits and maintenance needs of various pet breeds. You can live a happy, healthy life with your pet if you take the time to make this choice.

Chapter 3: Getting Your House Ready

Essential pet supplies

It's an exciting and happy event to welcome a new pet into your house, but it also needs careful planning to make sure that your new family member is secure, cozy, and well-cared for from the start. Getting the necessary materials for your pet is one of the most important parts of this preparation. This comprehensive guide will assist you in understanding and obtaining the supplies required for various pet breeds.

1. All-Pet General Supplies

No matter what kind of pet you choose, all pets need some fundamental supplies:

Food and Water Bowls: Sturdy, hygienic bowls are necessary. Heavy-duty plastic, ceramic, or stainless steel are all excellent choices. Make sure your pet's dishes fit properly in terms of size.

Identification Tags and Collars: In the event that your pet disappears, personalized ID tags with your contact details are essential. It's crucial that a dog's collar fits correctly; moreover, think about getting a leash or harness for your pet.

Pet Bed: Your pet will have a dedicated sleeping space with a cozy, supportive bed. Select a bed that fits your pet's size, and if cleaning is a concern, think about washable choices.

Grooming Supplies: Brushes, combs, nail clippers, and shampoo may be needed, depending on your pet's grooming requirements. Maintaining the health of your pet's skin and coat requires regular care.

Toys and Enrichment: Playing with toys helps you think clearly and get exercise. Select toys that are safe, long-lasting, and suitable for the size and species of your pet.

2. Dog-Specific Supplies

What you'll need in addition if you're taking a dog home is as follows:

Crate or Kennel: A crate is helpful for training and traveling, and it may provide your dog with a safe, secure place to live. Make sure your dog can comfortably stand, turn around, and lay down in the box.

Chew Toys: Because dogs naturally want to chew, you should provide them with a variety of chew toys to keep them entertained and prevent them from becoming destructive.

Training Supplies: Clickers, training pads, and treats are useful equipment for teaching commands and housebreaking pets.

Leash and Harness: For walks and other outside activities, a strong leash and harness are required. Compared to a collar, a harness is often more comfortable and offers greater control.

3. Supplies Particular to Cat

The following materials can assist you in creating a cat-friendly environment, since cats have specific needs:

Litter Box and Litter: Select a litter box that fits your cat's size and set it up in a discreet area that is easy to get to. Try out many kinds of litter to see which your cat likes most.

Cats must scratch in order to keep their claws in place and delineate their territory. To avoid causing damage to your furniture, provide scratching posts or pads that are strong.

Cat Tree or Perches: Cats enjoy climbing trees to get a good view of their surroundings. This urge may be satiated by wall-mounted perches or cat trees.

Carrier: When traveling or going to the vet, you need a safe, cozy carrier. Make sure there is enough ventilation and room for your cat to go around in.

4. Particular Provisions for small Mammals

Compared to dogs and cats, small animals like hamsters, guinea pigs, and rabbits have different needs:

Habitat or Cage: Provide a roomy cage with enough ventilation and bedding. Make sure the cage has hiding places and is impenetrable, so your pet feels safe.

Bedding and Nesting Materials: Make sure your bedding is safe and non-toxic. Shadings of pine and cedar should be avoided, as they may be toxic to small animals.

Exercise Equipment: For both mental and physical stimulation, chew toys, wheels, and tunnels are essential.

Feeding Accessories: For tiny animals, hefty, tip-resistant food dishes and water bottles with a sipper tube work well.

5. Specimen-Related Supplies

To guarantee their pleasure and well-being, birds need the following supplies:

Cage: Make sure the cage has adequate room for your bird to comfortably spread its wings and fly about. Bar spacing should be adjusted according to the size of your bird to avoid damage or escape.

Perches and Toys: To maintain the health of your bird's feet, provide a range of perches with varying textures and diameters. Playthings that promote problem-solving and foraging are particularly important for brain stimulation.

Food and Water Dishes: Cage bars connect to the dishes, making them safe and simple to clean. Make sure there is always fresh water accessible.

Bird Bath: To maintain clean and healthy feathers, birds love taking baths. Present a small bowl of water or a custom-made bird bath.

6. Specific Fish Supplies

 A distinct collection of materials is needed for fishkeeping in order to maintain a healthy aquatic environment.

Aquarium and Stand: Choose an aquarium that is the right size for the type and quantity of fish you want to keep. For the whole tank to be supported, a strong stand is required.

Filtration System: To preserve water quality and keep the tank clean, a dependable filtration system is necessary.

Heater and Thermometer: To keep tropical fish's water temperature constant, a heater is required. You can precisely check the temperature using a thermometer.

Use a water conditioner and test kits to eliminate dangerous contaminants from tap water. Test kits make it easier to keep an eye on water quality metrics, including pH, ammonia, nitrite, and nitrate levels.

Gravel and Decorations: To provide your fish with a stimulating habitat, choose decorations and gravel that are safe for aquariums. Both real and fake plants provide hiding places and improve the tank's appearance.

7. Reptile-Specific Supplies

To maintain their health and wellbeing, reptiles have certain demands that must be satisfied:

Terrarium: Pick a terrarium that will provide your reptile with enough room and ventilation. Think about the particular needs of a certain ecosystem, such as a tropical or desert area.

Substrate: Choose a substrate suitable for your reptile's species. Steer clear of substrates that, if consumed, may induce impaction.

Heating and illumination: In order to produce vitamin D3 and control body temperature, reptiles need certain temperature gradients and UVB illumination. When necessary, use UVB bulbs, under-tank heaters, and heat lights.

Hides and Climbing Structures: To provide a safe and engaging environment, including hiding places and climbing structures.

Feeding accessories: Tongs, feeding bowls, and live or pre-killed prey may be required, depending on the species.

Therefore, getting your house ready for a new pet requires careful preparation and obtaining the necessary items. You can facilitate a seamless transition for your new pet and provide the foundation for a happy, healthy life together by offering a secure, cozy, and engaging environment. Being a caring and loving pet parent requires spending time and money obtaining these necessary materials.

Establishing a Routine, Safe Areas, and Pet-Proofing

It's an exciting and fulfilling experience to welcome a new pet into your house, but it also needs careful planning to provide a secure and friendly space. Setting secure areas, pet-proofing your house, and setting a regular schedule for your pet are two essential components of this preparedness. This comprehensive guide will assist you in completing these crucial procedures.

Pet-proofing and Safe Places

A safe space is a place set aside, especially for your pet, to feel safe and at ease. This area offers your pet a haven when they're feeling anxious or overwhelmed, in addition to assisting them in acclimating to their new surroundings.

1. Selecting the Proper Location: Your pet's safe spot should be in a calm, low-traffic section of your house. This may be a nook in the kitchen or a part of the living area for pets. A quiet nook or an extra bedroom might be useful spaces for cats.

2. Soft Bedding: Set up a cozy bed or box with cozy bedding. Make sure it fits your pet properly in terms of size. While cats could choose a bed that is cushioned or even just a cardboard

box with a cover inside, dogs often prefer crates with soft blankets.

3. Necessary Supplies: Provide water, food, and toys, as well as other necessities, in the safe area. Provide a cat litter box that is situated apart from their food and drink bowl.

4. Privacy and Security: Make sure the space provides both privacy and protection from any threats. Newer pets may need some time to get used to living alone and away from noise and regular engagement.

Securing Your Home from Pets

Making your house secure from possible threats that might endanger your pet or damage your possessions is known as pet-proofing. The following actions will fully pet-proof your house:

1. Remove Dangerous Items: Keep medicines, chemicals, cleaning supplies, and other hazardous materials out of reach. If needed, store these things in cabinets with child-proof locks.

2. Electrical Safety: To avoid electrical shocks or fires caused by dogs chewing on wires and cables, cover outlets and conceal or fasten unsecured wires and cords.

3. Secure garbage bins: Make sure garbage can lids are tight to prevent dogs from rooting through them and swallowing dangerous items.

4. Plants: Recognize and get rid of any poisonous plants from your house. Common houseplants that may be dangerous or even fatal to pets include philodendrons, poinsettias, and lilies.

5. little Objects: Keep little items out of reach, including jewelry, change, and kid's toys. Pets have a tendency to chew on and swallow little objects, particularly puppies and kittens.

6. Pet Gates and Barriers: Use pet gates to prevent people from entering rooms that contain expensive or hazardous objects, kitchens, or stairs.

7. safe Windows and Balconies: To avoid falls, make sure windows have guards or barriers installed, and make sure windows have safe screens.

8. furniture and Decorations: Keep heavy, shaky furniture and décor objects secure so that pets can't fall on them or bump against them.

Establishing a Practice

Developing a regular schedule is essential for the health and happiness of your pet. It relieves stress and encourages good conduct by giving them a sense of security and a daily schedule.

Dining Schedule

1. Regular Feeding Schedule: Feed your pet at regular intervals throughout the day. This aids in controlling their

behavior and digestion. It's normal for dogs to eat twice a day, while cats could benefit from many little meals.

2. Nutritious food: Give your pet a well-balanced food according to their age, breed, and medical requirements. Request advice from your veterinarian on the ideal diet and feeding plan.

3. Clean Water: Make sure there is always access to fresh water. To avoid infection, clean the bowl often and change the water every day.

Workout and Recreation

1. Daily Exercise: Plan regular exercise sessions to keep your pet intellectually and physically engaged. Dogs need chances for running, playfulness, and frequent walks. Playing interactively with toys and climbing frames is beneficial for cats.

2. Mental Stimulation: Give your pet mentally stimulating toys, puzzles, and hobbies. To keep toys engaging, rotate them often.

3. Social Interaction: Engage in meaningful conversation with your animal companion. This might include just being in the same room, sharing a hug, or going through training sessions.

Education and Order

1. Consistent orders: When training, provide consistent cues and orders. This makes it easier for your pet to comprehend and comply with your instructions.

2. Positive Reinforcement: Give praise, goodies, or more time to play to encourage positive conduct. Your pet will repeat desired actions if they get positive reinforcement.

3. Set Boundaries: Clearly define the areas and activities that your pet is and is not permitted to engage in. To teach your pet to recognize and respect these boundaries, you must be consistent.

Sleep and Recuperate

1. Sleep routine: Establish a peaceful, cozy resting space to promote a regular sleep routine. The majority of pets will instinctively settle into a schedule that fits their owners' way of life.

2. Nap Times: Admit that pets—especially young ones like puppies and kittens—need plenty of relaxation and naps throughout the day. Make sure they have a peaceful, unoccupied location to relax.

Sanitization and Health

1. Regular Veterinary Visits: Make time for routine veterinarian examinations to keep an eye on your pet's health and ensure that all immunizations are current.

2. Grooming Schedule: Decide on a schedule for grooming that is suitable for the breed and requirements of your pet. This may include washing, brushing, and cutting nails.

3. Parasite Prevention: Guard your pet from fleas, ticks, and other parasites by taking preventative steps. To find out the finest products and procedures, speak with your veterinarian.

So,There's more to getting your house ready for a new pet than simply purchasing supplies. Establishing a regular schedule that supports your pet's physical and emotional well-being is just as important as creating safe areas and pet-proofing your house. By doing these things, you can make sure that your house is a safe and friendly place for your new friend, laying the groundwork for a long and happy life spent together.

Chapter four: The Adoption Process

Getting a pet may bring unlimited enjoyment and companionship into your life, making it a beautiful and rewarding experience. However, it's imperative that you approach the adoption process with consideration and readiness. This guide will help you through the key steps of the adoption process, including where to find your pet, what questions to ask before adopting, and what to expect on the first visit.

Breeders, shelters, and rescue groups are some places where you may find pets. There are many places where you can adopt pets, each with its own advantages and disadvantages. The following is a summary of the primary sources:

1. Animal shelters
Animal shelters are nonprofit establishments whose mission is

to care for and place stray animals in new homes. They look after a variety of animals, including dogs, cats, rabbits, and more.

Some advantages include the following:
Wide Selection: Animals at shelters often represent a range of ages, sizes, and breeds.
Lower Cost: Adopting a pet from a shelter usually entails a lower down payment than buying from breeders and generally includes basic veterinary care like vaccinations, spaying/neutering, and microchipping.
Saving a Life: Adopting from a shelter helps reduce the number of homeless dogs and prevents animals from being put to death.

Considerations:

Health and Behavior: While most dogs at shelters are in excellent health, some may be suffering from behavioral issues or undetected medical ailments. Shelters frequently conduct health assessments, but it's crucial to understand any identified issues.
Background Information: Animals at shelters may have had hazy or short histories, especially if they were stray.

2. Manufacturers of animals

Breeders are individuals or organizations dedicated to creating a certain kind of animal companion. Choosing a reliable breeder will help ensure that the animal you buy has a traceable history and pedigree.

The Advantages are :

Predictability: Breeders may provide detailed information on the breed, temperament, and any health issues with the pet.

Early Socialization: Pets purchased from breeders often get early care and socialization, which may facilitate their transfer to new homes.

Cost: Pets from breeders may be far more expensive than animals from rescues or shelters.

Ethical Considerations: It is crucial to choose a responsible breeder that prioritizes the health and wellbeing of their animals. Avoid puppy mills and unethical breeding practices.

3. Rescue Organizations

Rescue organizations focus their efforts on protecting certain animal types or varieties. They often operate via a network of foster homes.

Specific Breed: If you're looking for a certain breed but would like to adopt rather than buy from a breeder, rescues are fantastic.

Foster Care: Rescue organizations frequently place their animals in foster homes, where they receive customized care and training that makes it easier for you to understand their requirements and behavior.

Considerations

Procedure for Adoption: Purchasing a pet from a rescue may include a more rigorous process that includes home visits and extensive paperwork to ensure the adoptive family is a good match.

Availability: Breed-specific rescues may always have fewer animals than shelters.

Issues to Think About Prior to Adopting

Before adopting a pet, it's important to gather as much information as you can to ensure that you're making the best decision. The following are crucial questions to ask:

1. Requests for Shelters and Rescues

Health History: What is the pet's past medical history? Have they been vaccinated, microchipped, and spayed or neutered?

Behavioral Assessment: What aspects of the pet's temperament and behavior are known to you? Are there any acknowledged issues, like animosity, anxiety, or fear?

Background: Can you tell us about the pet's past? Were they found to be stray animals, transported from another facility, or handed in by a previous owner?

Daily Care: How often does the pet currently get fed, exercised, and groomed? Are there any specific dietary needs or restrictions?

Compatibility: How well-mannered is the animal with children and other pets? Does the place where the pet lives need to fulfill any specific requirements?

Support: What kind of post-adoption help does the shelter or rescue offer? Do they provide training, behavioral issues, or health difficulties services?

2. Questions for Breeders

Breeding Practices: Could you describe your conception and breeding procedures in more detail? How can you ensure the wellbeing and happiness of your animals?
Parent Information: Can I get to know the pet's parents? What is their health status and temperament?
Health Guarantees: What health guarantees or warranties do you provide? How do you feel about genetic testing and health examinations?
Socialization: How do you socialize your kittens or puppies? What kind of early education or background do they have?
References: Do you have any endorsements from previous clients? Exist any easily available reviews or endorsements?

The first consultation

The first meeting with your potential new pet is one of the most significant and thrilling stages of the adoption procedure. During this visit, you may interact with the pet, observe their behavior, and decide whether they would be a good match for your home and lifestyle. Here are a few tips for getting the most out of your trip, as well as some things to prepare for:

1. Reading the Visit Report

Research: Learn as much as you can about the breed or kind of pet you're thinking about getting. Acknowledge their needs, habits, and any potential obstacles.

List of Questions: Based on the pet's profile and your specific concerns, compile a list of questions. Never be scared to delve thoroughly into your pet's past, behavior, and overall health.

Dysfunctional Families: If at all possible, bring along any other family members or pets who will be living with the new animal. This ensures everyone is comfortable and aids with compatibility assessment.

2. Monitoring and Acquainting Oneself with the Pet

Behavior: Observe the pet's actions under various conditions. Are they shy, playful, apprehensive, or confident? Watch how they react to different stimuli, such as strange faces or loud noises.

Interaction: Have a discussion with your animal partner. Play with them or spend time with them as you watch how they respond to your voice and touch. This helps you figure out who they are and how comfortable they are with you.

Wellness Assessment: Look for physical signs of health issues, such as a clean, clear eye, a healthy coat, and good mobility. Ask about any problems you see.

3. Assessing the environment

Living Conditions: When it comes to shelters and rescues, be mindful of the institution's condition and hygiene. You may use this to determine the level of care the animals get.

Home of the Breeder: For breeders, check the conditions in which the pets live. Are they kept in clean, spacious quarters?

Do they have access to socialization and physical activity?

4. Reaching a Conclusion

Comfort Level: Consider your level of comfort with the pet and the facility. If anything seems off, go with your instincts, take some more time, or go elsewhere.

Follow-Up Visits: Consider carefully before making a choice. It's often a good idea to arrange many visits to ensure that the pet is a suitable fit and to see how their behavior changes over time.

The process of adoption calls for careful preparation, research, and planning. Knowing where to search for your pet, being prepared with the right questions before adoption, and making the most of the first visit can ensure a successful and fulfilling adoption experience. Despite the effort and commitment involved in acquiring a new pet, the joy, companionship, and unwavering love they provide make it an incredibly rewarding experience. If you take the time to be ready for this new chapter in your life, you and your new furry (or feathered, or scaled) friend might enjoy a happy and healthy relationship.

Chapter 5: Your New Pet's First Adjustment Period

Adopting a new pet means making a big adjustment for both you and your new friend. Since it lays the groundwork for your pet's comfort, trust, and behavior in their new surroundings, the first adjustment phase is very important. Three crucial facets of this time will be covered in this guide: acclimating your pet to their new residence, fostering trust and a strong relationship, and managing typical behavioral problems.

Establishing a Secure and Cozy Environment

1. Designated Area: To begin, keep your pet confined to a certain room or area within your house. This smaller area keeps them from feeling overwhelmed by the unfamiliar

surroundings and helps them feel safe. Provide everything this space needs, including a bed, dishes for food and drink, toys, and a cat litter box.

2. Slow Discovery: Allow your pet to gradually investigate the remaining areas of your home. You may extend their access to other locations as they get used to it. Thanks to this progressive approach, they can adjust at their own pace and have less worry.

Introducing Members of the Household

1. Family Introduction: To avoid overwhelming your family, introduce your pet to each household member one at a time. Permit the pet to approach each individual and sit quietly. Steer clear of abrupt movements and loud sounds.

2. Other Pets: Take care to introduce your new pet to your current pets gradually and under supervision. First contacts should be short and under supervision. When allowing pets to view and smell each other without coming into actual contact, use barriers like baby gates. They should gradually extend their time together as they grow more at ease.

Creating Schedules

1. Regular Routine: Make sure that feeding, walking, playing, and bedtime are all done on a regular basis. Pets want consistency, so having a set routine makes them feel safe and comfortable.

2. House Training: This is a crucial part of caring for puppies

and kittens. Frequently take them to their designated toilet place, particularly after meals, throughout the night, and when they wake up. When they make it to the restroom successfully, give them praise and treats.

Improving the Environment

1. Toys and Activities: To keep your pet engaged both intellectually and physically, provide them with a selection of toys and activities. Interactive play, puzzle toys, and chew toys all help to prevent harmful tendencies and boredom.
2. Safe Spaces: Make sure your pet can escape and unwind in designated areas. For cats, they might be high perches or hiding places. A comfortable box or a peaceful nook with a bed might serve as a dog's safe haven.

Fostering Bonds and Trust

1. Rewarding excellent conduct: To show your pet appreciation for excellent conduct, use positive reinforcement tactics. Affection, praise, and treats may help foster trust and encourage desirable behavior.
2. Consistency: The secret to successful training is consistency. When you want certain behaviors, use the same signals and instructions. Particularly when it comes to rescued animals that may have been abused or neglected, exercise patience and kindness.

Time Spent Together in Quality

1. Interactive Play: Spend extended periods of time with your pet. Playing interactively improves your relationship and gives you the necessary workout. Make use of toys that replicate your pet's natural activities, such as fetching and tug-of-war for dogs or chasing and pouncing for cats.
2. Love and Care: Show your pet love by giving them attention, patting them, and conversing with them. Observe their nonverbal cues and consider their comfort level. It might take some dogs longer than others to become receptive to tactile love.

Confidence Building

1. Exposure to New Experiences: Introduce your pet to people, places, and experiences on a gradual basis. Positive exposure lowers their anxieties and fears while boosting their confidence.
2. Calm and Reassurance: In unfamiliar or potentially tense situations, maintain your composure and provide comfort. Because your pet looks to you for clues, keeping your composure will make them feel more safe.

Managing typical behavioral problems

Divorce Anxiety

1. Gradual Departures If your pet exhibits symptoms of separation anxiety, practice gradual departures and

returns. Begin by letting them alone for brief periods of time, then progressively extend that time.

2. Comfort Items: Give your pet something to cuddle with while you're gone, such as a favorite toy or a piece of clothing.

3. Safe Space: Make sure they have a cozy, safe area where they feel at ease on their own.

Indoor Soiling

1. Regular Routine: To control your pet's bowel movements, maintain a regular feeding and potty routine.

2. Supervision and Confinement: Keep a tight eye on your pet while it is being housebroken. When you are unable to keep an eye on them directly, confine them to a confined space.

3. Positive Reinforcement: Congratulate and treat your pet after they use the restroom successfully. Rewarding mishaps should be avoided, as they might engender worry and terror.

Damaging Gnawing and Biting

1. Appropriate Outlets: Provide chew toys and scratching posts as suitable outlets for biting and clawing.

2. Deterrents: To prevent destructive activity, use deterrents such as protective covers or bitter sprays for furniture.

3. Redirecting Behavior: If you see your pet biting or

clawing anything improper, refocus their attention on acceptable objects. Give them praise for utilizing the right tools.

Aggression

1. Identifying Triggers: Recognize and comprehend the things that make your pet act aggressively. Fear, resource guarding, and territorial behavior are common causes.
2. Expert Assistance: If your pet's aggressiveness continues or presents a concern, get expert assistance from a licensed veterinarian or a certified animal behaviorist.
3. Desensitization and Counter conditioning: Use desensitization and counterconditioning methods to modify your pet's reaction to stimuli. This entails praising calm conduct while introducing the trigger to them gradually and under supervision.

Overindulgent Meowing or Barking

1. Understanding the Cause: Determine what is causing the excessive vocalization. It could be brought on by worry, boredom, attention-seeking, or health problems.
2. Training and stimulation: To lessen anxiety and boredom, provide mental and physical stimulation. Teach your pet to obey quiet orders, and give them treats when they behave calmly.
3. Schedule and Comfort: To manage anxiety-related vocalization, maintain a regular schedule and provide

comfort.

Your new pet's first few weeks of acclimation are a period of change and exploration. You can help your pet settle into their new home and form a strong, loving connection by providing a secure and comfortable environment, encouraging positive interactions that foster trust and bonding, and skillfully managing typical behavioral problems. To ensure a smooth transition phase and a happy, peaceful existence with your new furry (or feathery, or scaled) family member, patience, consistency, and understanding are essential.

Chapter six: Pet health and well-being

Responsible pet ownership is really about ensuring your pet's health and well-being. This entails locating a trustworthy veterinarian, arranging for routine examinations and shots, offering a healthy diet, and keeping up with grooming and cleanliness. Your pet will live a long, healthy, and happy life if they get complete medical treatment and wellness support. This comprehensive guide will help you take care of your pet's medical and wellness requirements.

Locating a Veterinarian: Selecting the Appropriate Practitioner

1. Research and suggestions: Begin by looking for local veterinarians. Consult with loved ones, friends, or other pet owners for advice. Online evaluations and rankings may also provide insightful information about the quality of treatment

that various veterinarians offer.

2. Credentials and specializations: Verify the veterinarian's licensure and possession of the required qualifications. Certain veterinarians specialize in treating exotic animals, dermatology, or orthopedics. Select a veterinarian whose specialization matches the requirements of your pet.

3. Facility Tour: Take a look around the veterinary clinic to evaluate the general layout, order, and cleanliness. A state-of-the-art clinic with up-to-date equipment is necessary to provide top-notch treatment.

4. Communication and rapport: Choose a veterinarian who is easy to understand and will take the time to address your concerns. Having a positive relationship with your veterinarian is essential for talking about your pet's health and resolving any issues.

5. Emergency Services: Find out whether there are any emergency services available. It's important to know where to go if an emergency occurs after business hours or if your pet needs immediate treatment.

Building a Bond with Your Veterinary Professional

1. First Visit: Arrange a visit to introduce the veterinarian to your pet. During this appointment, your pet may become acquainted with the clinic setting, and the veterinarian can do a baseline health evaluation.

2. Medical History: Give a thorough account of your pet's past

medical conditions, surgeries, shots, and prescription drugs. This information is critical for accurate diagnosis and therapy.

3. Open Communication: Keep in contact with your veterinarian in an honest and open manner. Talk to your veterinarian about any changes in your pet's health, temperament, or appetite, and heed their advice for any preventative care and treatments.

Frequent medical exams and vaccinations

The Value of Frequently Scheduled Exams

1. Early Detection of Health Issues: Frequent veterinarian examinations make it possible to identify any health problems early on. Early management may improve the prognosis for a number of diseases and prevent mild issues from becoming more severe.

2. **Health Change Monitoring**: Regular examinations assist in keeping an eye on how your pet's health changes over time. This is crucial for elderly dogs in particular, as they are more likely to acquire chronic illnesses that need constant care.

3. Preventative treatment: Dental cleanings, parasite control,

and weight management are examples of preventative treatment that may be arranged during checkups. Preventive care may prolong and improve your pet's quality of life considerably.

Vaccines

1. "Core Vaccinations": Vaccinations against common and possibly deadly illnesses are a must for all dogs. The basic vaccinations for dogs usually consist of adenovirus, parvovirus, distemper, and rabies. The key vaccinations for cats are feline herpesvirus (rhinotracheitis), feline calicivirus, feline distemper (panleukopenia), and rabies.

2. Non-core immunizations: Depending on your pet's lifestyle, surroundings, and risk factors, non-core immunizations are advised. Lyme disease, leptospirosis, and bordetella (kennel cough) vaccinations are examples of non-core immunizations for dogs. Bordetella and the feline leukemia virus (FeLV) are examples of non-core vaccinations for cats.

3. Vaccination plan: Follow your veterinarian's recommended immunization plan. A series of immunizations is usually required for puppies and kittens beginning at 6–8 weeks of age, with booster shots every 3–4 weeks until the animals are 16–20 weeks old. Regular booster injections are necessary for adult dogs to maintain immunity.

Diet and Nutrition

Well-Rounded Diet

1. High-Quality Pet Food: Feed your pet a healthy, well-balanced food that is appropriate for their size, age, species, and state of health. Select premium commercial pet food that satisfies the dietary guidelines set out by reliable institutions like the Association of American Feed Control Officials (AAFCO).

2. Life Stage Nutrition: Adjust the diet to suit your pet's life stage. While adult dogs need maintenance meals, puppies and kittens need increased protein and calorie intake for development. Diets designed to improve joint health, weight control, and cognitive function may be beneficial for senior dogs.

3. Special Dietary Needs: Due to medical issues like diabetes, renal illness, or allergies, many dogs require a specific diet. To find the ideal diet for treating these illnesses and to make sure your pet is getting the right nutrients, speak with your veterinarian.

Schedule for Feeding and Position Control

1. Portion Control: To avoid obesity and overfeeding, measure the quantities of food given to your pet. As you assess your

pet's activity level and physical condition, make adjustments to the feeding schedule specified on the pet food container.

2. Feeding routine: Make sure your feeding routine is regular. Feeding your pet twice a day is recommended for most pets; however, this might change depending on their age and condition. Free-feeding should be avoided since it might result in overeating and weight gain.

Surfactant

1. Fresh Water: Make sure your pet always has access to clean, fresh water. Sustaining body function and preserving general health depend on enough water.

2. Water Intake Monitoring: Keep an eye on your pet's water intake since variations may point to underlying medical conditions. Reduced thirst might be linked to sickness or dehydration, whereas increased thirst can indicate illnesses like diabetes or renal disease.

Personal Care and Washing

1. Brushing: Regular brushing minimizes shedding, keeps your pet's coat in good condition, and keeps matting at bay. Your pet's coat determines the type and frequency of brushing. Short-haired breeds may just need weekly brushing, whereas long-haired breeds could need daily brushing.

2. Bathing: Use pet-safe shampoo and give your pet a bath as needed, usually every 4–6 weeks. You should follow your

veterinarian's advice on your pet's individual needs, since overbathing may deplete the coat of natural oils and irritate the skin.

3. Nail cutting: In order to avoid overgrown nails, which may lead to discomfort and movement problems, regular nail cutting is necessary. Using the proper nail clippers or a grinder, trim your pet's nails every two to four weeks, or as required.

Oral Health

1. Teeth Brushing: Use toothpaste and a toothbrush that is safe for pets to brush their teeth on a regular basis. Strive for twice-a-day brushing to avoid plaque accumulation and lower your chance of dental illness.

2. Dental Chews and Toys: Offer toys and dental chews that enhance oral health. These may help keep your pet's teeth clean by reducing plaque and tartar.

3. Expert Dental Cleanings: As required, consult your veterinarian to arrange for expert dental cleanings. Scaling and polishing are used in these cleanings to get rid of plaque and tartar that at-home treatment is unable to eliminate.

Tear and Optical Care

1. Ear Cleaning: Frequently examine your pet's ears for indications of infection, accumulation of wax, or dirt. Using cotton balls or pads and an ear cleanser that the veterinarian

recommends, clean their ears. Cotton swabs should not be used, as they might harm the ear canal.

2. Eye Care: Check for redness, discharge, or cloudiness in your pet's eyes. To carefully remove any debris or tear stains, use a moist towel. If you notice any indications of eye problems, see your veterinarian.

Coat and Skin Care

1. Parasite Control: Guard your pet from fleas, ticks, and other parasites by taking preventative steps. Products like collars, oral pills, and topical treatments might be recommended by your veterinarian.

2. Skin Health: Keep an eye out for lumps, redness, or irritation on your pet's skin. Healthy skin and a glossy coat are facilitated by regular grooming and a balanced diet. If you notice any persistent skin issues, consult a veterinarian.

A comprehensive strategy is needed to maintain your pet's health and welfare, including selecting a reliable veterinarian, planning regular examinations and immunizations, feeding them a balanced diet, and making sure they are groomed and cleaned properly. By giving these caregiving responsibilities top priority, you can promote your pet's overall health and well-being and help them have a happy and fulfilled life. Keeping up with your veterinarian's demands and having regular conversations with them are critical to providing your furry friend with the best treatment possible.

Chapter seven: Your Pet's Socialization and Training

Good pet care requires good socialization and training. These procedures help guarantee that your pet has a happy and satisfying existence, learns basic instructions, behaves correctly in a variety of settings, and develops excellent manners. The fundamentals of training and socialization are covered in detail in this book, including housebreaking and learning basic instructions, interacting with humans and other dogs, and offering mental stimulation and enrichment.

Fundamental instructions and home training

For both your peace of mind and your pet's safety, it is imperative that they learn to obey simple orders. The following fundamental commands are essential for every pet to learn:

1. Sit:
Purpose: Educates your pet to sit on demand, a basic skill that eases anxiety and encourages serenity.
Teaching Method: Place a treat near your pet's nose, then raise your hand such that their head follows the goodie and their tail touches the ground. Say "Sit," give them the reward, and offer them praise after they are seated.

2. Remain:
Purpose: Maintains your pet stationary, which is essential for safety and behavior control in a variety of settings.
How to Teach: Have your pet sit down at first. Take a few steps back, open your palm to them, and say, "Stay." If so, give them a treat and some encouragement. Increase the time and distance gradually.

3. Enter:
Purpose: An essential instruction to ensure that your pet returns to you, especially in potentially hazardous circumstances.
How to Teach: Put your pet on a leash, call them over, and gently nudge them in your direction. When they get to you, give them a reward and some appreciation. Practice in several settings to help you remember the instructions.

4. Down:
Purpose: Encourages your pet to lay down upon request, which may aid in hyperactivity management and foster a state of calm.

How to Teach: Allow your pet to smell a goodie that you are holding in your closed palm. Slide your hand along the ground, then move it to the floor when they follow. Say "Down," hand them the reward, and give them praise when they lay down.

5. Go Away:

Purpose: Keeps your pet from snatching or consuming anything dangerous.

How to Teach: Allow your pet to smell a goodie that you are holding in your closed palm. Say "leave it" and offer them an alternative reward. Placing the treat on the ground and covering it with your hand will gradually increase the difficulty.

In-Home Instruction

To make sure your pet knows where and when to relieve themselves, house training is a must. Whether you have an adult pet, a puppy, or a kitten will affect the procedure significantly, but the fundamentals will always be the same.

1. Set Up a Schedule:

Consistency: Whenever possible, take your pet outdoors or to their designated toilet location, particularly after they've eaten, drunk, woken up, or played.

Timing: Adult pets can retain their urine longer than puppies and kittens, which may need to go outside every hour due to their tiny bladders.

2. Assign a Spot for Potty:

Specific Spot: Let your pet release themselves in a reliable location. They will be reminded of the right location by the comforting aroma.

Supervision: Walk with your pet to the appropriate spot and stay there until they do potty. Give them a prize and commendation right away.

3. Encouraging Reward:

Rewards: Confirm successful potty breaks with love, praise, and snacks. Rewarding behavior encourages repetition.

Accidents: After any mishap, do a thorough clean-up to get rid of any residual odor. Reprimanding someone may generate dread and worry.

4. Training in Crates:

Safe Space: Since most dogs don't sabotage their sleeping quarters, crates may be a useful tool for house training. Make sure the box is the right size, with enough space for the animal to stand, turn around, and lay down.

Gradual Introduction: Fill the cage with toys and goodies to create a happy and comfortable environment for your pet. At first, use the box for short bursts of time, then gradually extend its use.

Getting Along with People and Other Pets

Your pet needs socialization to grow up to be a well-adjusted, self-assured, and amiable being. Aggression, anxiety, and fear are less likely to occur with proper socializing.

1. *Key phase:* For pups, the key socialization phase is between 3 and 14 weeks, and for kittens, it is between 2 and 7 weeks. Introduce your pet to a range of people, creatures, places, and activities during this period.

2. *regulated exposure:* Gradually expose your pet to new situations in a pleasant and regulated way. Gradual exposure keeps things from overwhelming them and guarantees a good conversation every time.

A Brief Overview of Other Pets

1. Neutral Territory: To avoid territorial behavior, introduce your pet to another animal in a neutral setting. A park or other open space is perfect for dogs. A different room in the home may be suitable for cats.

2. monitored interaction: Make sure all early exchanges are monitored and short. To maintain control over the situation and stop any violent behavior, use obstacles or leashes.

3. Positive Reinforcement: Give both animals praise for their composure and good manners. As they get more at ease with one another, they gradually lengthen and increase the frequency of their encounters.

Interacting with Individuals

1. Variety of People: Take your pet to interact with a range of people, including women, men, kids, and senior citizens. This helps them feel comfortable around a wide variety of people.

2. Calm Setting: Make sure the first few exchanges happen in a composed and safe environment. To foster good relationships, encourage others to approach your pet gently

and provide rewards.

3. Handling and Touching: Acclimate your pet to being touched and handled by various individuals. This is especially crucial for veterinarian appointments and grooming.

Good social reactions

1. Training lessons: Sign up for socialization or training lessons for your pet. These courses teach vital skills and provide scheduled socializing opportunities.

2. Play Dates: Set up playdates with other canine companions. Make sure the size, age, and temperament of the two animals are appropriate, and that they are both at ease.

3. Public Outings: Take your pet to parks, pet shops, and outdoor cafés, among other pet-friendly public spaces. They are exposed to various settings and stimuli during these excursions.

Mental Enrichment and Stimulation

Enrichment and mental stimulation are essential for your pet's general health. Providing mentally stimulating activities for them lowers anxiety, avoids boredom, and encourages a happy and healthy lifestyle.

Active Playthings

1. Puzzle Toys: These toys test your pet's problem-solving skills. These toys often include concealing kibbles or treats, which your pet has to learn to collect. They are a great source of cerebral stimulation and long-term pet employment.

2. Chew Toys: Sturdy chew toys give dogs a cerebral exercise in addition to satisfying their innate need to chew. Select toys that are appropriate for your pet's size and chewing style while remaining safe.

Skills and Techniques

1. Advanced Training: After your pet has mastered the fundamentals, introduce them to more complex maneuvers and behaviors. Their relationship is strengthened, and their brains are kept occupied by this ongoing training.
2. Positive Reinforcement: Make sure your pet enjoys training sessions by using positive reinforcement strategies to promote learning. To keep them interested, keep your sessions brief and entertaining.

Old Games

1. Nose Work: Dogs especially love scent activities that make use of their keen sense of smell. Treats should be hidden throughout the home or yard for your dog to locate. Their innate hunting instincts are satisfied, and their minds are stimulated by this action.
2. Interactive Feeders: To make mealtimes more interesting, use interactive feeders or toys that dispense treats. By making your pet struggle for their food, these feeders slow down their eating and provide them with mental activity.

Improving the Environment
1. Varied Environments: To keep things fresh, sometimes switch up your pet's surroundings. To pique their interest,

rearrange furnishings, add new toys, or designate distinct play spaces.

2. Outside Exploration: Let your pet explore parks, nature trails, and your backyard, among other outside spaces. Supervised exploration feeds their innate curiosity while stimulating their senses.

Social Engagement

1. Playtime: Give your pet frequent opportunities to play with toys, games, and other things they like. Playing interactively improves your relationship and gives you the necessary mental and physical activity.

2. Social Visits: Schedule frequent social get-togethers with humans and other animals. Good social relationships save people from being lonely and bored while also stimulating their minds.

Ordinance and Framework

1. Regular Schedule: Adhere to a regular daily schedule for eating, playing, sleeping, and exercising. A feeling of security and anxiety reduction are provided by predictability.

2. Well-Stimulated Activities: Offer a harmonious blend of cerebral stimulation, physical activity, and rest. Adapt exercises to your pet's specific needs and preferences.

A pet's upbringing involves socializing and training in order to guarantee that it learns appropriate conduct, adjusts to new surroundings, and has a happy, healthy existence. You can help your pet become a well-mannered, confident, and content member of your family by providing mental stimulation and enrichment, concentrating on housebreaking and basic instructions, and socializing with other pets and humans. Training a pet requires a lot of patience, consistency, and positive reinforcement.

Chapter eight: Long-Term Things to Think About When Owning a Pet

Making future plans

You make a lifelong commitment to their care and welfare of your pet when you welcome them into your house. This commitment entails future planning, scheduling travel and pet sitting, and thinking through end-of-life care. By being aware of these long-term factors, you can make sure your pet has the greatest life possible at every step of their development.

Money Management

1. Budgeting for Expenses: Maintaining a pet has recurring expenses, including supplies, toys, food, veterinarian care, and grooming. Make a budget that covers both unforeseen medical crises and these ongoing costs.

2. Pet Insurance: To assist in controlling the expense of veterinarian treatment, think about purchasing pet insurance. Depending on the coverage, pet insurance may cover sickness, accidents, and even normal care. Look into several plans to choose one that meets both your financial requirements and the demands of your pet.

3. Emergency Fund: Set aside money from your emergency fund specifically for your pet's needs. This fund may be used to pay for unforeseen expenditures like emergency surgery, medical treatments, or other unanticipated bills.

Regarding Housing

1. Pet-Friendly Housing: If you rent your property, make sure your lease allows pets. Certain landlords set limitations on the kinds and sizes of pets that are allowed. When relocating, take the pet policies into account.

2. Space and Environment: When selecting a pet, take into account your living area and surroundings. Smaller pets or cats could feel more at home in an apartment, while larger dogs might need more room and access to a yard.

3. Future Moves: If you're thinking about moving in the future, consider how your pet will react to it. Make plans for a seamless move by investigating pet-friendly housing alternatives in prospective new places.

Modifications to Lifestyle

1. Family Changes: Think about how your pet could be impacted by changes in your family's dynamics. A new baby's birth, a marriage, or the departure of a family member may all affect your pet's routine and behavior. To reduce tension, schedule gradual introductions and modifications.

2. Career Changes: Your ability to spend more time with your pet may be impacted by job changes that include longer hours or more travel. Think about how you will take care of your pet's requirements if your work schedule changes; you may want to hire a dog walker or pet sitter.

Legal Aspects

1. Identification and Microchipping: Make sure your pet is properly identified, preferably with a collar with ID tags and a microchip. In the event that your pet becomes lost, this helps bring them back to you.

2. Pet Trusts and Wills: If you have a pet, think about including it in your will or establishing a pet trust. This legal agreement guarantees that, in the event of your incapacitation, your pet will be taken care of. Choose a dependable individual to take care of your pet and supply the funds necessary to meet their demands.

Pet and Travel Sitters

Taking your pet on vacation

1. Preparation and Planning: Make sure your pet is at ease in a vehicle or other kind of transportation before you go. As you gradually adapt to travel, take brief excursions to see how comfortable they are.

2. Travel Essentials: Bring food, water, bowls, a leash, a carrier or box, bedding, and any prescription drugs your pet may need. Bring copies of their health records, which should include their immunization history.

3. Pet-Friendly Accommodations: If you want to stay overnight, find out which lodging options allow pets. Pets are accepted at many hotels, motels, and vacation rentals, but it's advisable to check the specifics of their rules and any extra costs.

4. Travel Safety: Use a pet seatbelt harness or a secure container to protect your pet while they are traveling. It is never a good idea to leave your pet alone in a parked vehicle because the temperature could suddenly drop.

Researching Pet Sitters

1. Expert Pet Sitters: If you require in-home care for your pet while you're away, consider hiring a professional pet sitter. Professional sitters may provide individualized care and are qualified to manage a variety of pet care duties.

2. Friends and Family: Assign your pet's care to dependable friends or family members. Make sure they understand your pet's routine and any special requirements.

3. Pet Boarding: If you'd rather not leave your pet at home, look into reputable boarding establishments. By paying a visit in advance, you can ensure that the facility meets your needs and provides a secure and cozy space for your pet.

4. Pet Care Directions: Provide thorough directions on how to take care of your pet, including feeding schedules, how to provide medications, how to exercise, and who to call in case of an emergency. Add any particular preferences or behavioral oddities your pet may have.

Dying with Dignity

Identifying Aging Signs

1. Health Monitoring: As your pet ages, regular veterinarian examinations are crucial for keeping an eye on their health. Pay attention to any changes in their general health, appetite, mobility, or demeanor.

2. Comfort and Quality of Life: Evaluate the level of comfort and quality of life for your pet, taking into account things like pain, mobility, and activity tolerance. For advice on how to treat any chronic diseases or pain, speak with your veterinarian.

Take care of the dying

1. Pain Management: In collaboration with your veterinarian, create a pain management strategy for your pet. This might include giving your pet medicine, physical therapy, or other comfort-enhancing procedures.

2. Environmental Adjustments: Modify your house to suit your senior pet's needs. Provide comfortable bedding, convenient access to food and drink, and remove any barriers that may make it difficult to move about.

3. Emotional Support: Give your pet comfort and love throughout the times you spend together. Pets benefit from your friendship and confidence, particularly older animals.

Decisions on euthanasia

1. Veterinarian Consultation: To find out when it would be appropriate to think about euthanasia, speak with your veterinarian. They may offer advice based on your pet's condition, degree of suffering, and overall quality of life.

2. Making the Decision: Choosing to put a cherished pet to sleep is a very tough choice. Think about your pet's best interests as well as your veterinarian's recommendations. Recall that making this decision may be a kind approach to stopping suffering.

3. Dear Pet: Make sure their last moments are spent in a calm and cozy environment. Surround them with people you love and things they know well. A lot of vets provide in-home

euthanasia services, so your pet may die in the comfort of their own house.

Focus and Memorialization

1. Burial or Cremation: Select your preferred method of final resting place. These services are provided by some vet offices, or you may choose a pet cemetery or crematory.

2. Memorializing Your Pet: Do something to pay tribute to your pet's memory. Think about putting together an album of pictures, planting a tree, or giving money to a pet charity in their honor.

3. Grieving and Support: Give yourself permission to mourn your pet's passing. For assistance, consult your loved ones, friends, or pet loss support organizations. It's important to allow yourself the time and space you need to recover from grief, since it's a personal process.

The long-term aspects of pet ownership include future planning, scheduling trips, pet sitting, and becoming ready for end-of-life care. By foreseeing and taking care of these issues, you can ensure that your pet gets the care and attention they need for the remainder of their life. When the time comes, you may grant your pet a dignified and peaceful death while also helping them to enjoy a full and happy life with thoughtful preparation and loving care.

Conclusion

Considering the journey of owning a pet

Taking up pet ownership is a significant and transformative experience. As soon as you make the decision to adopt a pet, you assume responsibility for another living creature. This is a trip full of trials, treasures, and priceless lessons.

The first joy and difficulties

There is no feeling like the thrill you get when you bring a new pet home. The first few days are exciting and full of new experiences, whether you acquire a calm adult pet, a rambunctious puppy, or an inquisitive kitten. During this period, you will also have to deal with issues such as housebreaking your pet, acclimating them to their new surroundings, and creating a schedule. These provide the basis for your pet's behavior and health and are essential for creating a deep relationship with them.

The Strengthening Link: Days become months, and your relationship with your pet becomes closer. You begin to comprehend their distinct personalities, inclinations, and peculiarities. Routines become second nature, and the early difficulties transform into beloved habits. Having a pet by your side makes you feel better, less stressed, and full of happiness and laughter. Pets form gratifying and soothing relationships with us because of their amazing capacity to feel our emotions and provide us with unconditional affection.

Getting Past Obstacles: You will face a variety of challenges with your pet during their lifetime, ranging from behavioral disorders to health concerns. These difficulties put your endurance, fortitude, and dedication to the test. To overcome these challenges, one needs commitment, empathy, and perhaps expert assistance. Every obstacle overcome deepens your relationship and reinforces the enormous responsibility that comes with pet ownership. On this voyage, you learn tolerance, compassion, and the value of constancy and affection.

Continuous Education and Adjustment

Having a pet requires ongoing learning. Your pet's requirements and habits will alter as they get older. Whether it's changing their food, updating their fitness regimen, or offering extra medical treatment, you adjust your care plan to meet their changing needs. A pet owner teaches you to be proactive, flexible, and aware of your surroundings in order to protect your companion.

The Path of Emotions: The emotional experience of having a pet is quite gratifying. Pets provide us with company, teach us empathy and responsibility, and give us a fresh perspective on life. They are happy in the good times and comforting in the bad. A pet and owner have a deep emotional bond and make memories that will last a lifetime.

Having a pet is a lifelong commitment that calls for constant learning and adjustment. It's crucial to use a variety of learning materials to make sure you're giving your pet the finest care possible.

Veterinary Advice

1. Regular Check-ups: Form a rapport with a reputable veterinarian who can provide routine check-ups as well as guidance on behavior, diet, and preventative treatment.

2. Specialist Consultations: When dealing with certain health conditions, seek the counsel and treatment of veterinary experts, such as dermatologists, cardiologists, or behaviorists.

Resources for Behavior and Training

1. Expert Trainers: Seek the assistance of expert trainers for socialization, behavior modification, and obedience training. Trainers may provide specialized guidance and methods tailored to your pet's specific needs.

2. Online Tutorials and Courses: Make use of webinars, tutorials, and online courses covering a range of topics related to pet behavior and training. Online materials are widely available from a variety of credible organizations and educators.

Reference books for teachers

1. Books and E-books: Invest in books that talks about pet. These publications may provide in-depth information on a variety of subjects, including nutrition and health, pet care, and training.

2. Periodicals and journals: Get up-to-date information on trends, research, and best practices in pet care. Experts in the field frequently contribute articles to these magazines.

Online forums and communities

1. Pet Forums: Join online groups and forums where pet owners can exchange stories, advice, and encouragement. These networks link you with other pet owners who could be dealing with similar issues and provide a plethora of useful information.

2. Social Media Groups: Join and follow social media accounts dedicated to pet care. These communities often provide insightful advice, anecdotes, and updates on pet care techniques.

Seminars and workshops

1. Local Workshops: Take part in seminars and workshops on training, health, and pet care that are held locally. These gatherings provide opportunities for interactive learning, question-asking, and expert interaction.

2. Virtual Seminars: A lot of companies provide webinars and virtual seminars, which make it simple to pick the brains of professionals without having to leave your house.

Programs for Rescue and Shelter

1. Adoption Programs: Rescue groups and shelters may frequently provide resources and assistance to new pet owners. They could provide behavior therapy, health advice, and training sessions.

2. Community Outreach: Take part in events like spay/neuter clinics, vaccination campaigns, and pet care seminars that encourage responsible pet ownership.

Ongoing Veterinary Training

1. Veterinary organizations: Be informed about the latest policies and suggestions from veterinary organizations, such as the British Veterinary Association (BVA) and the American Veterinary Medical Association (AVMA).

2. Research papers: To keep up with the most recent developments in pet health and care, read research papers and case studies that have been published in veterinary journals.

Being a pet owner is an amazing and fulfilling experience. It calls for a combination of love, endurance, dedication, and lifelong learning. You can make sure you're giving your pet the best care possible by taking the time to think back on the trip, recognizing the practical and emotional components, and making use of the tools that are available to you.

In return, your pet will provide you with years of devotion, love, and company. It's important to keep in mind that growing, comprehending, and cherishing the link between you and your pet are all part of the journey through the many phases of pet care.

Having a pet is a lifetime commitment that is very fulfilling and joyful. You can provide your pet with a secure, caring, and stimulating environment for the duration of their life by establishing future plans, scheduling travel and pet sitting, and thinking through end-of-life care. To guarantee that your pet has a happy, healthy, and well-cared-for life, you should reflect on the trip and never stop looking for information and resources.

Accept the journey, draw lessons from the setbacks, rejoice in the victories, and savor each and every second spent with your cherished pet. Every effort and sacrifice is justified because of the special and irreplaceable link you have with your pet.